THE NEW TRADITIONAL

BARCLAY BUTERA

THE NEW TRADITIONAL

BARCLAY BUTERA

FOREWORD BY PHIL HANEY

GIBBS SMITH
TO ENRICH AND INSPIRE HUMANKIND

FOR MY MOTHER

FOREWORD

BY PHIL HANEY
PRESIDENT AND CEO, LEXINGTON HOME BRANDS

The power of design resonates within each of us on an emotional level. Those with a passion for design approach the process as a journey that begins with a flash of inspiration and grows into something remarkable. I have the greatest admiration for design professionals who can walk in their clients' shoes, listen to their aspirations, interpret that vision through the lens of their own creativity, and deliver a stunning look that elevates the clients' view of their own personal style.

Barclay Butera is one of those rare talents, gifted with the ability to interpret dreams on the canvas of interior design. It begins with his capacity to foster relationships and manifests itself in visually inspiring spaces that are transformational for his clients. I have watched the evolution of his aesthetic over the last twenty-five years, marveling at his ability to reinvent the look of new traditional style. His diverse body of work encompasses every possible style category, yet there are always classic design elements that ground the look with a comforting sense of familiarity.

In 2017, we launched an initiative for Barclay to collaborate with Lexington on a portfolio of signature collections. With three design studios, a staff of twenty-five designers, and projects from the Hamptons to Maui, Barclay has his finger on the pulse of the luxury market in a way that very few do. More importantly, his gift for interpreting traditional style in a fresh, relevant, and aspirational way is without equal. Barclay's designs make a sophisticated statement while retaining the spirit of casual elegance that makes them intimate and approachable.

For me, the highlight of our successful business relationship has been entirely personal. I have learned why Barclay is so gifted in connecting with clients. His sincerity, authenticity, and humility foster an immediate sense of trust. That trust and rapport serve as a foundation for the creative process. The projects showcased in this book offer a glimpse into the amazing diversity of his designs.

A national editor once described Barclay's work as "unbuttoned elegance." To me, that is the essence of his signature style. If the heartbeat of great design lies in bringing inspiration to life, the industry has no finer ambassador, no greater talent, and no better friend.

HARBOR ISLAND

PHOTOGRAPHY BY MANOLO LANGIS

Built on an exclusive private island in Newport Beach, this five-bedroom, seven-bathroom home is defined by its stateliness. The three-story waterfront architectural feat boasts stunning harbor views and a dock with accommodations for multiple sailing yachts. We were brought onto the project by the homeowner and instantly had a clear vision for how the interior furnishings would be crafted. As firm believers that the architecture begins the conversation that the interiors carry out, we were honored to take part in telling this home's story. Once we decided we wanted this home to be rooted in classic design, we were able to bend and break the rules to bring forward what was lasting and beautiful for the clients.

The interiors are characterized by an all-American grandeur that pays homage to the large, sprawling estates of the New England Coast. Oftentimes, the structure and location set the stage for the interiors, and this was absolutely the case for Harbor Island. Clean-lined, upholstered silhouettes and elegant, sophisticated details are found throughout. The palette was inspired by the colors of the ocean and fit the traditional yet contemporary style of the home perfectly. Designing spaces that captured the essence of the family that would soon call it home was a priority. The open-concept floor plan includes a bar, lounge, great room, dining room, and kitchen in the main living space. To create spatial definition, each space was grounded with generously sized custom rugs. Rich character was folded in with textural materials and beautiful heirloom-quality furnishings.

Refined elegance and sophistication are in perfect harmony in the primary suite. Vaulted ceilings add height to the primary bedroom, while the furnishings create a cozy atmosphere. The magnificent windows are perfectly positioned to capture views from every room. Double twelve-foot vanities in the primary bath add grandeur, while the sky-blue flowering branch wall-covering adds a whimsical touch.

It is important to note that new traditional approach is about breaking the rules of design and creating innovative solutions for each unique project. Beautiful, inspiring spaces have the ability to create a profound effect, and I'm constantly fascinated by the idea of creating a piece of art in which to live. All in all, this residence is timeless and seamlessly bridges the gap between past and present.

FIRST IMPRESSIONS

Upon entering the 8,300-square-foot home, you are greeted by a 30-foot foyer that opens up to all three stories. American black walnut hardwood floors with a mosaic inlay pattern of African wenge wood instantly announce the grandeur of the home.

"ONCE WE DECIDED WE WANTED THIS HOME TO BE ROOTED IN CLASSIC DESIGN, WE WERE ABLE TO BEND AND BREAK THE RULES TO BRING FORWARD WHAT WAS LASTING AND BEAUTIFUL FOR THE CLIENTS."

CLEVER INCLUSION

The front door and steel windows line up perfectly with the steel grid that makes up the wine cellar and glass elevator. The first two levels of the home boast twelve-foot ceilings, which were made possible only by digging the foundation four feet below the ground level, all completed by Patterson Custom Homes and Brandon Architects.

EXECUTIVE STUDY

In the study, intricately carved ceiling trellis details juxtapose
herringbone floors and medium-toned wood-paneled walls.

ELEVATE THE EVERYDAY

An ebonized mahogany writing desk with a leather inset sits opposite two wood-trimmed

chairs upholstered in a deep teal wool to bring in a pop of color to the space.

"BEAUTIFUL, INSPIRING SPACES HAVE THE ABILITY TO CREATE A POWERFUL EFFECT, AND I'M CONSTANTLY FASCINATED BY THE IDEA OF CREATING A PIECE OF ART IN WHICH TO LIVE."

GATHERING SPACE

This house is all about light, and we designed the placement of the furniture around capturing the best views.

Club chairs upholstered in a luxurious velvet create a conversational lounge adjacent to the first-floor bar.

PERFECT BALANCE

Opposite: The first floor lounge offers an informal yet luxurious entertaining area to enjoy cocktails and conversation all while taking in the oceanfront setting.

Above: Handsome details abound in the executive study's private powder room. Rich wood paneling, moody coastal art, and a textured wallcovering envelop the space.

"LASTING INTERIORS DO NOT RELY SOLELY ON FURNITURE AND DÉCOR ALONE. A CLEAR DIALOGUE MUST TAKE PLACE BETWEEN THE ARCHITECTURE AND DESIGN ELEMENTS."

BONUS ROOM

The third-floor game room gives the owners additional space to entertain friends
and family in an intimate, private space that leads to the rooftop deck.

GREAT HEIGHTS

Vaulted ceilings add height to the primary bedroom. It was paramount to scale each
furnishing proportional to the space. The addition of wallpaper above the wood paneling
helps bring warmth to the tall ceilings.

GROUNDING AND ELEVATING

Harbor Island is where the refined and grand coexist in a setting that can't be duplicated.

"THE ARCHITECTURE BEGINS THE CONVERSATION THAT THE INTERIORS CARRY OUT."

MARIGOLD

PHOTOGRAPHY BY NATHAN SCHRODER

Hired as a referral from dear clients, we worked on this project in the seaside village of Corona del Mar for a busy professional couple who were relocating to California from Florida. The home would become the primary residence for the couple and their adult children, and when we first visited the property, we knew it would require a full renovation. We took the house down to the studs, removing dark paneling, small windows, tiled countertops, and dated cabinetry. Though the house felt very heavy and dark, its footprint had potential and the location couldn't be beat.

The clients were eager to update the home from its original Tuscan style to create a modern coastal look that fit the locale. By inventing the structure, we were able to breathe life back into the home and bring it up to date for this modern family. Having their complete trust in us to deliver a beautifully designed home, the process could not have gone smoother.

With 2,800 square feet to work with, we hand-sketched the layout of each room and optimized every square inch. First, we reimagined the formerly dark kitchen and opted for a waterfall countertop with gray and white veining to achieve a light and bright openness that the home did not previously possess. A 60-inch range was a must-have item for the couple, as they love to cook and entertain. Handblown blue glass pendants topped it all off and act as jewelry for the space.

In an effort to accentuate the beauty of the staircase, we finished the handrail in glass and designed the wine cellar under the stairs in a steel and glass enclosure. Soft blues and celadons float throughout the home, with the ocean as inspiration for the color palette. A custom sectional in a durable fabric grounds the living room, while various coastal landscapes and textiles add richness and reflection that keep the mood light and airy.

On the second floor, a double-sided fireplace enrobed in a creamy white wave porcelain adds movement and opens up the room. Materials including glass, metal, and European oak were added throughout the home. A signature touch of mirrors behind the nightstand in the primary bedroom opens up the room as if we had added windows to the space.

The rooftop is the crowning achievement, with 360-degree views and a partially covered outdoor living space. Everything in the home is a highly personal expression of the homeowners' tastes, and we happily succeeded in bringing their vision to life.

PROPORTION AND MOVEMENT

We focused on streamlined proportions and refined aesthetics that meld well with the bones of the structure. The open-concept floor plan in the dining and sitting area offers ample seating.

"REIMAGINING THE FORMERLY DARK KITCHEN, WE OPTED FOR A WATERFALL COUNTERTOP WITH GRAY AND WHITE VEINING TO ACHIEVE A LIGHT AND BRIGHT OPENNESS THAT THE HOME DID NOT PREVIOUSLY POSSESS."

BLUE AND WHITE

Opposite: Original coastal art is found in a secondary bedroom. A classic white duvet allows the opportunity to change out pillow textiles frequently.

Above: The minimalist kitchen features a waterfall island and a stunning glass and wood staircase.

TEXTURE AS ART

The wavy, pure white ceramic surface tells a beautiful story and acts as an
art form in the primary bathroom. A double-sided fireplace adds depth to
the space and separates the bedroom from the bath.

PEACEFUL FEELING

The door and window frames were selected to blend seamlessly with the sand-colored European white oak flooring. Earth tones and rich textures define the primary bedroom, which features an oversized balcony with ocean views.

FAMILY FRIENDLY

Leather ottomans on casters tuck under the custom cocktail table in the living area. The space also features natural materials such as a woven chair and nesting end tables of petrified wood.

CONTINUITY

Opposite: An outdoor seating area appointed with an upholstered sectional and fossilized clam shell coffee table offers a private area to relax in the sunshine.

Above: A teak dining table and sleek, white sling chairs continue the modern traditional feel in the outdoor living area. Ledger stone was selected for the exterior of the home, including the fireplace in the loggia.

ARDEN ROAD

PHOTOGRAPHY BY RYAN GARVIN

Inspired by the old Pasadena architecture reminiscent of a bygone era, we began work on this beautiful new build with a transitional classic look in mind. The home was perched on an expansive half-acre lot and had more than 5,000 square feet of living space. We had completed two vacation homes for our clients in nearby locales and were tasked with designing the interior and exterior of their newly built primary residence—a compliment in its own right. We couldn't wait to get our hands on the two-story home situated in a charming neighborhood on a tree-lined street. Truly speaking to our axiom of "client for life," the family was a joy to work with and we set out to create a home that was unlike any of the others before.

A home should embrace the people within it and reflect their tastes, values, and preferences. For this family of four with young children, we worked with the architect to provide ample spaces for equal parts homework and play. Relying on our quintessential blue and white palette, we infused new takes on fabrics and materials to give it a fresh and current look. The media room, complete with a midnight-blue grass cloth, is roomy with a larger-than-life sectional for the whole family to pile in on movie nights. In the bedrooms, we utilized a soft, pale blue palette with silver accents. The great room has an equestrian flair and opens up to the pool and backyard, while the covered outdoor living areas offer airy space for easy entertaining. Verdant landscaping and mature trees line the property, providing ample privacy and allure.

This family knew exactly what they wanted, and bringing their vision to life was an intoxicating process from start to finish. We were able to deliver a fresh and crisp look, as the majority of the furnishings were bespoke custom pieces designed specifically for their new space.

> "A HOME SHOULD EMBRACE THE PEOPLE WITHIN IT. THE SPACES WE CREATE AIM TO REFLECT THEIR TASTES, VALUES, AND PREFERENCES."

CLASSIC WITH A TWIST

Opposite: Traditional design elements including symmetry and balance were utilized in the dining room and sitting area.

Above: Matching sideboards and upholstered lounge chairs were placed in a conversational setting, anchored by a rock crystal chandelier with gold highlights.

EQUESTRIAN NOD

The beautiful white millwork acts as a blank canvas accented by classic stained-wood bookshelves in the living room. Designed with unfussy materials, including rich leather and a deep blue linen, this space is elegant enough for formal entertaining and relaxed enough for children to enjoy.

WELL STYLED

Floor-to-ceiling glass doors open onto the lush green garden and pool area. The focal point of the room is an equestrian-influenced three-tier chandelier finished in polished nickel and chocolate leather.

"OUR GOAL WAS TO MARRY FORM AND FUNCTION WHILE KEEPING IT VERY GLAMOROUS."

PATTERN PLAY

Known for our clever use of pillows, we paired a floral, stripe, and geometric print to make the sectional sing. Darker wood tones and furniture bring balance to the space.

BEAUTY REIGNS

The kitchen and dining area are appointed with white cabinets, continuous marble slab countertops, and polished nickel hardware and plumbing fixtures.

"I AM FASCINATED BY THE IDEA THAT WHAT IS NEW IS ACTUALLY BASED IN THE PAST."

CHINOISERIE CHIC

An exquisite hand-painted wallpaper hangs in the primary bath. Reminiscent of floral 18th-century Chinese designs, the wallpaper truly is a work of art and complements the unique vanity that is painted in robin's-egg blue and finished with antique hardware.

SERENE SOPHISTICATION

A bedside table in the primary suite is adorned with an intricate trellis design and hand-appliqued silver leaf. A classic blue-and-white cachepot holding a flowering orchid is juxtaposed by a modern sculptural alabaster table lamp.

"I LIKE TO REFER TO THE OUTDOOR LIVING SPACE AS THE 'FIFTH ROOM.' IT SHOULD BE AS GLAMOROUS YET AS COMFORTABLE AS ANY INDOOR OPTION."

EASY ENTERTAINING

In the media room, we kept the patterns to a minimum and instead built layers with textures to create a warm and inviting experience. The navy fabric and wallcovering are not only tactile but add the perfect color layer to awaken the space.

RENEW AND REFRESH

Nestled on a spacious lot, this contemporary classic estate exemplifies modern living with traditional elements
that reflect the homeowners' diverse tastes and background.

OUTDOOR LIVING

Designed with effortless entertaining as well as privacy in mind, the backyard features tall hedges and a generously sized swimming pool with a calming water feature.

"WHEN SOMETHING IS WELL DESIGNED IT SHOULD MAKE YOU FEEL GOOD AND WE ACHIEVED JUST THAT FOR OUR CLIENTS."

ONE SNOWMASS

PHOTOGRAPHY COURTESY OF EAST WEST PARTNERS

Jumping at the opportunity to design the model residence at One Snowmass, Aspen, we created an alpine-chic ski retreat for our clients, developers East West Partners. A mid-century modern mountain sensibility infused with natural warmth rounds out this two-bedroom condo at the base of Snowmass Mountain. Opting for a striking yet unexpected color palette, we selected rich jewel tones as a counterpoint to the light interior walls and wood finishes. Architectural floor-to-ceiling glass windows allow both nature and natural light to be drawn into the home. The contemporary aesthetic pairs with the grandeur of both the spacious interior and the sweeping mountain views from every room.

An oversized, metal-clad fireplace in the great room serves as a focal point and adds visual interest to the space. Luxurious gold and emerald pillows add dimension and texture to the snowy white sofa, while a polished concrete coffee table anchors the room, creating a comfortable and elegant gathering space. Illuminating the great room in a halo of diffused light is an exquisite, three-tier, aged-bronze chandelier. In the kitchen, all of the appliances are fully integrated and wood paneled, creating a harmonious flow in the open-concept floor plan. A dramatic black agate wall mural takes center stage in the dining room, while the polished walnut table with hints of brass adds a classic flair.

The primary bedroom suite features a sprawling outdoor deck and is perfect for dining al fresco and taking in the picturesque views of the Elk Mountain Range. The colorful geometric wallpaper and striking wall décor in the twin guest bedroom is both unexpected and unique.

The finished result is an exceptionally designed modern mountain home with sophisticated furnishings and décor pieces that speak to the surrounding environment. It defies the expectation of a rustic mountain home and proves that contemporary can be classic. One Snowmass is a place to entertain and relax with friends and family while soaking up the beauty of all four seasons.

NEUTRAL AND IMPACTFUL

Opposite: In the dining room, a dramatic black agate wall mural takes center stage, while the polished walnut table with hints of brass tie in with the linear brass hanging fixture.

Above: Clean lines and knotty, unfinished cabinetry link the kitchen to the natural landscape.

MODERN MOUNTAIN

In the living room, jewel tones are simple but luxurious. Gold and teal pillows add dimension and texture to the creamy white sofa, and a polished concrete coffee table anchors the room, creating a comfortable and elegant gathering space.

"A NEW DESIGN GENRE WAS INVENTED FOR RESIDENTS OF ONE SNOWMASS, A PRIVATE SKI IN-SKI OUT ENCLAVE OFFERING MIDCENTURY MODERN LIVING WITH AN ALPINE–CHIC AESTHETIC."

ROOM WITH A VIEW

Opposite: The contemporary furnishings are perfectly paired with the grandeur of both the spacious interiors and the majestic views of snowy mountaintops through floor-to-ceiling windows.

Above: Winters at One Snowmass are equally as beautiful as summers, and residents are able to take advantage of the remarkable views year-round from the primary bedroom.

"THE COLORFUL GEOMETRIC WALLPAPER AND STRIKING WALL DÉCOR IN THE GUEST BEDROOM ARE BOTH UNEXPECTED AND UNIQUE."

WOW FACTOR

Above: In the guest bedroom, twin beds upholstered in a blue velvet contrast with the gold and rust-orange palette. Bold original art adds a touch of whimsy to the space.

Opposite: Simple fixtures and a floating, streamlined vanity add to the minimalist look of the primary bath.

PROMONTORY

PHOTOGRAPHY BY DOUG BURKE

Situated in a private mountain community on 6,400 acres of land overlooking iconic Park City, Utah, Promontory stands as a one-of-a-kind mountain escape. The custom-built cantilevered structure seems to defy gravity, and the interiors mimic the jaw-dropping architecture. After several years of vacationing in the mountain town, our clients decided to make a permanent commitment and purchased the property ready to break ground. Joining the project in the early phase of construction allowed us to hand select the finishes and materials, which was so pivotal to the design direction.

Avid art collectors and outdoor enthusiasts, the owners wanted a home that would push the envelope and stand in a class of its own. Iterations of striking jewel tones, eye-catching sculptural furniture, and playful patterns reflect both their style and personality. The pursuit of form and meticulous detailing were the driving factors of the exquisite and bespoke design. The homeowners love that the home is suited to their lifestyle, habits, and needs, embracing the surrounding nature and retaining all of the elements of the outdoors.

The home is beautifully crafted, and there is a level of discovery and intrigue found around every corner. We painstakingly sourced unique pieces that fit the home perfectly and stand alone as talking points. Take, for example, the green granite in the primary bath, sourced locally from a quarry in the Wasatch Range. Some rooms are monochromatic in composition, while others highlight a style of their own, offering surprise and delight.

Incorporating the best elements of a legacy mountain estate, this home is eclectic yet harmonious and is an exercise in authenticity. Being very deliberate with our design selections, we achieved an overall look that is uniquely compelling. An eye-catching juxtaposition of "old meets new" persists throughout the home where streamlined pieces meet natural materials. The owners couldn't be happier and truly love spending time here, where they can slow down and enjoy the pace that Utah has to offer.

"THE PURSUIT OF FORM AND METICULOUS DETAILING DRIVE THE EXQUISITE DESIGN OF THIS BESPOKE HOME."

GRAND ENTRANCE

Sculptural lighting and the use of unexpected materials and silhouettes are key factors in making the living room one of a kind. In this larger-than-life home, it was also paramount to design with scale in mind.

ARCHITECTURAL DETAILS

The beautiful shapes of the custom furnishings create an atmosphere that is glamorous yet comfortable and inviting at the same time. Equally drawn to the orderly beauty and sculptural simplicity of modern design, we composed a look that incorporates both elements.

INFORMAL FORMALITY

The pieces in the home were hand selected and exude a beautiful yet accessible feel. An oversized sectional anchors the room, while a linear, black honed-granite fireplace extends almost the full length of the wall.

LUXE AND MODERN

The open-concept kitchen is at once luxe and modern with a large scale that's perfect for entertaining. Marrying dark wood cabinetry with a delicious marble slab and gold finishes creates a sleek, elevated look. Elegant glass and gold open shelving is a nod to the style of French bistros.

MODERN ESCAPE

The first floor was designed primarily for ease and enjoyment. A full bar, lounge area, and wine cellar offer all the trappings of a members-only club. Designing this home truly felt like creating a work of art.

AGED TO PERFECTION

The temperature-controlled wine cellar features rich wood detailing in a herringbone pattern. No detail was overlooked, and each and every decision played an important role in achieving the final atmosphere.

PALETTE

Leaning into the warm, earthy hues of the natural surroundings, we incorporated a rich velvet swivel chair that makes it easy to take in the views through the floor-to-ceiling windows.

NATURAL BEAUTY

Opposite: A freestanding, honed Brazilian solid soapstone tub takes full advantage of the sweeping views. We added unexpected bronze details through the fixtures and texture through the reeded cabinetry.

Above: in the primary bedroom, the landscape influenced the selection of muted earth tones and natural textures.

COMPOSITION

The modern architecture and rustic natural surroundings forge a dynamic interplay. The monochromatic composition of the exterior building materials, including glass and metal, highlights the hues and textures found in the landscape.

PARK MEADOWS

PHOTOGRAPHY BY KATE OSBORNE

Newly built in the only private golf and social club in the heart of Park City, Park Meadows is a luxury area in a resort town. Our design for this majestic home utilizes a monochromatic palette to blend old and new. Set on a spacious lot, the property exudes a sense of calm from the moment you turn into the driveway.

Our clients, full-time residents of Park City, preferred a subdued, clean aesthetic that was mindful of the surroundings and took into account the way the home fits into the natural landscape. The homeowners were drawn to midcentury modern silhouettes that had a traditional quality to them. We let nature influence the color palette, opting for creamy whites and soothing gray-blues that work well in both the winter and summer light. Drapery treatments play an important role in creating a magical cocoon-like feel throughout the home. Surprising accents of bold color surface on small items such as pillows and vases and add a sense of playfulness and richness.

A custom, neutral wool rug anchors the living room, while a cocktail table in polished white stone and brass balances the ample seating. To add drama to the dining room, we installed an extravagant midcentury brass-and-glass Sputnik chandelier above a reclaimed-wood dining table. In the primary bedroom, our clients requested a peaceful setting that was modern but not cold or stark. A channel-tufted headboard accented by aged-brass nightstands achieved the feel. Because of the streamlined bones of the home, we left it to the accessories to add a sculptural quality.

Design elements throughout the house blur the line between classic and contemporary, and we confidently achieved the perfect marriage of beauty and functionality. With its effortless luxury, Park Meadows is an ethereal mountain sanctuary. Ultimately, this chic, contemporary residence is exactly what the owners envisioned for their home.

"ONE OF THE KEY INGREDIENTS TO A WELL-STYLED SPACE IS TRAYS. NOT ONLY DO THEY HELP CORRAL ITEMS IN A BEAUTIFUL, ARTFUL WAY, BUT THEY WORK ORGANIZATIONAL WONDERS FOR ANY ROOM IN THE HOME."

TOUCH OF COLOR

Layers of texture and plush upholstery transform the living room into a coveted destination for lounging and mingling.

MAGNOLIA MUSE

When it came to creating a beautiful and inviting space, modern silhouettes with bold accent pieces gave this mountain home a sleek, streamlined look.

"THIS CHIC, CONTEMPORARY RESIDENCE IS UNFUSSY AND EXACTLY WHAT WE ENVISIONED FOR THE OWNERS."

MONOCHROME

A little escape from everyday life, the sitting room is accented with

natural elements and a striking marble texture painting.

"DESIGN SHOULD BE THE PERFECT MARRIAGE OF BEAUTY AND FUNCTIONALITY."

PAIRING ACCESSORIES

A pair of hurricanes in two different heights add dimension to the end table.

SUBTLE PATTERN

Opting for a more subdued color palette, we incorporated fun vintage textiles that tell a beautiful story.

STATEMENT PIECE

Above: The dining room called for an extravagant midcentury modern Sputnik fixture that steals the show.

Opposite: In the kitchen, an oversized waterfall island with plenty of space for food prep, storage, and dining creates handsome, modern lines with the sleek cabinetry beyond.

"THE MASTERFUL USE OF A MONOCHROMATIC PALETTE BLENDS OLD AND NEW."

LOUNGE EASY

The bespoke upholstered swivel chairs feature softly curved lines.

GOLDEN GLIMMER

A beautiful burst of gold shines through in a chandelier from the owner's collection.

WATERCOLOR DREAMS

Above: In the corner of the primary bedroom, a jewel-toned lounge chair and ottoman add a striking contrast to the crisp white walls.

Opposite: Sometimes the smallest spaces are the best for making bold design statements. Dreamy lavender-and-blue cloud wallpaper infuses a soft, watercolor quality, while modern gold fixtures sparkle in the powder room.

SAGE CREEK

PHOTOGRAPHY BY NATHAN SCHRODER

Nestled beneath a sea of terra-cotta rooflines and California olive trees, sits a 7,800-square-foot Santa Barbara Spanish home, just waiting for us to reinvigorate the spirit of the interiors. The estate overlooks the unspoiled natural beauty of the surrounding coastal mountain region and has a quiet serenity that washes over you the minute you step foot on the grounds. Our goal was to design the home from the outside in and create a comfortable retreat to celebrate the relaxed glamour of California's past for the young family of four.

We first met our clients at our Newport Beach showroom when they stumbled upon the drawings of a project we were presenting and fell in love with the luxe material palettes and thoughtful detailing. They had just moved into their home and, although it had appealing features, the interiors were missing key design elements and left something to be desired.

The Santa Barbara architecture dictated the interiors, and we gave new life to the traditionally darker selections by lightening everything up. Room by room, we reconceptualized the entire floor plan and brought every detail up to par. Subtly textured rugs, throws, wallcoverings, and draperies in a restrained palette of celadon, pale blue, and sand are peppered throughout the home. Challenged with incorporating existing pieces from our client's previous home, we mixed and matched the new with the old. New pillows in energetic patterns and colors freshened up drab spaces and added new life to the rooms. In the guest casita, the combination of color, art, and light all come together in perfect harmony to create a warm and unified space.

To finish off the project, we made additions to the backyard, including revamping the courtyard and outdoor living areas complete with a custom shade structure and seating groups on all three sides of the home. We transformed the property into a comfortable and classic estate with a design that feels as natural as the setting. Every exacting detail was thought of, down to the trim on each pillow, and the result is a breathtaking home that our clients truly enjoy.

HEIRLOOM QUALITY

Opposite: The entryway features an arched barrel ceiling and rich walnut floors.

Above: Understated elegance reigns supreme in the dining room.

SETTING THE SCENE

An air of relaxed formality can be found in the living room. Rich wood floors and beams as well as arched windows and doors add an extra dimensional layer.

CLASSIC ELEMENTS

Above: Utility without sacrificing style was high on the priority list for the kitchen. Numerous drawers and clever spaces to store everyday items are concealed behind classic white cabinetry. Gray-blue leather stools with silver nailhead detailing are tucked under the Calacatta marble island.

Opposite: In the breakfast nook, a custom banquette upholstered in a slate linen complements the rectangular farmhouse table.

ALL ABOUT LIGHT

Above: A perfectly restrained aesthetic and subdued palette was incorporated into the upstairs sitting room.

Opposite: Luxurious custom bed linens complete the look of the client's son's bedroom.

PRIMARY SUITE

Opposite: An elegant sitting area nestled against the natural landscape features custom chairs, an oak accent table, walnut-stained floor lamps, and a circular tufted ottoman atop a vintage Turkish rug.

Above: A tufted headboard in the primary bedroom adds a discerning feel.

ULTIMATE SANCTUARY

Double vanities flanking the freestanding soaking tub and a floral-patterned mosaic in soft grays forge a rich, textural palette in the primary bath.

"THE COMBINATION OF COLOR, ART, AND LIGHT FALL TOGETHER IN PERFECT HARMONY TO EVOKE THE FEELING OF SERENITY."

GUEST RETREAT

Opposite: A dramatic antique silver mirror-and-glass pendant is the focal point just past the arched entryway of the casita.

Above: A series of botanical prints in the guest retreat hang above a custom teal sofa.

"THE CREATIVE USE OF A MULTITUDE OF MATERIALS, INCLUDING LIMESTONE, BRICK, TRAVERTINE, AND MARBLE, TRULY MAKES THIS AN ORIGINAL SPACE."

CALIFORNIA COOL

Taking advantage of the Mediterranean climate of Southern California, we maximized the outdoor spaces, turning the side yard into a bocce ball court and adding a custom-built teak outdoor table with seating for ten.

GLENEAGLES

PHOTOGRAPHY BY NATHAN SCHRODER

Our clients, whose primary home is two hours inland in Pasadena, fell in love with Newport Beach and desired a formal yet relaxed seaside escape. Symmetry was the crowning design principle found throughout, and we did not hold back when it came to indulging our clients with the most luxurious surroundings.

In the entry, a striking round pedestal table topped with blue-and-white vintage ginger jars, tea canisters, and vases from the Far East sets a tone of luxury. Ebony-stained floors contrast with the mostly neutral furnishings of the home and serve as a grounding, polished force. The formal living room features ceiling-height drapery, and upholstered linen sofas flank the fireplace. In the dining room, gold gilding is ever present and a double-pedestal table with Chippendale chairs is centered on a window overlooking the garden. In the kitchen, where more casual entertaining takes place, a trestle table surrounded by wicker and cerused wood chairs upholstered in a light blue gingham welcomes friends and family to linger just a little longer over breakfast.

In terms of paint, we wanted something somewhat unexpected, and the shade of blue we achieved looked as though it could have been original to the residence—an old-world color that worked wonderfully throughout the primary bedroom and bath. The soft blue paint covers the entirety of the walls and millwork, while celadon silk Roman shades and panels drape the windows. Inspired by the French way of living, the primary bedroom features a white-painted writing desk, sparkling crystal chandelier, fireplace, and linen settee at the foot of the bed.

The primary bath, complete with a white-and-gray marble bathtub, is at once opulent and understated. Style was not sacrificed as we continued the French blue color palette from the bathroom into the bedroom.

In the end, a relaxed elegance was achieved, where the homeowners can unwind and revel in the beauty of the classic design.

ELEGANCE DEFINED

Above: Collected vintage ginger jars, tea canisters, and vases from the
Far East are displayed in the foyer on a large center table.

Opposite: An antique French secretaire from the couple's collection sits
on the right of the ornately designed plaster fireplace surround.

"WE WANTED THIS SPACE TO EXUDE THE STYLE OF A FRENCH SALON BUT ALSO CONFORM TO THE WAY THE OWNERS LIVE TODAY."

SUBLIME GATHERING PLACE

Opposite: A shimmering crystal chandelier presides over the dining table, while the chairs exude the utmost refinement with cushions tied with silk tassels.

Above: The breakfast area in the family kitchen is fitted with an antique wood refectory dining table and upholstered blue-and-white gingham chairs.

"THERE WAS A REAL DESIRE BY THE HOMEOWNERS TO ESTABLISH A FORMAL YET RELAXED ENVIRONMENT."

LIGHT AND SPACE

Above: An airy space with an extraordinary quality of calm and light, the primary suite has touches of French influence and is enrobed in a beautiful blue hue.

Opposite: Struck by the beauty and simplicity of an antique console table, we converted it into a vanity in the guest bathroom.

A TOUCH OF FORMALITY

Above: In the dressing room, a marble center island glistens beneath a crystal chandelier.

Opposite: An oversized gilded lantern in the guest bedroom anchors the room while an antique white painted twin bed adds a feeling of refined elegance to the space.

VIA STRADA

PHOTOGRAPHY BY NATHAN SCHRODER

Dreaming up a desert retreat for longtime clients was an exercise in letting the natural landscape and architecture guide the design. Inspiration lies everywhere in nature, and particularly here in La Quinta, California, where we embraced the surroundings to truly give this home a distinct and personal style. The home's location on the golf course, with panoramic views of the San Jacinto Mountains, made the project uniquely compelling and influenced the design direction.

Our clients were very descriptive with how they envisioned their second home and brought imagery and concepts to relay their ideas. Being avid art and antique collectors, they were instrumental in shaping the personality of this space—noticeably exemplified in the gentleman's office, where we wrapped the walls in a deep teal and grounded the space with the client's ornately carved, seventeenth-century Portuguese writing desk. Their unique perspective made what we dreamed up even that much better. The home boasts an edited palette of medium to light wood and clean white paint. They wanted all the comforts of traditional design elements but with a contemporary feel that embraced their outdoor lifestyle of golfing, swimming, and playing tennis.

In the living room, the proportion and scale are drawn from the architecture, and the furniture placement was designed to create balance and multiple entertaining areas. Textures are found throughout the home, from the woven fabrics to the grain of the floors. Subtle touches of color are folded in with textiles, wallpaper, art, and accessories. The loggia serves as an extension of the living room, with woven chairs and a limestone fireplace connecting the indoors with the outdoors.

We paid great attention to detail when selecting the lighting and each piece tells a unique story. The dining table and chairs resemble antiques and mingle with the client's art and accessories. The primary bedroom features soft, textured wallpaper walls and a white tufted velvet bed, bringing elegance to this well-appointed sanctuary.

The result is a very special home that honors the architecture, landscape, and most importantly, our clients. This home represents the richness of luxury desert living, and the homeowners could not have been more pleased.

"I TRULY VALUE WORKING WITH EACH OF MY CLIENTS. THEY BRING A UNIQUE PERSPECTIVE THAT MAKES WHAT I DREAM UP EVEN BETTER."

LUSHLY APPOINTED

Opposite: In the living room, a two-tier nickel chandelier hangs from aged white oak beams running perpendicular to the backyard. We contrasted minimal white walls with the beams to amplify the weight and warmth of the material.

Above: Wide plank wood flooring transitions to polished travertine in the loggia. Both are finished in a similar tone for a cohesive feel. It was extremely important for us to connect the home to the mountainous desert landscape and the peaceful feeling of being on the golf course.

LET THE LIGHT IN

Opposite: Another angle of the main living area illustrates the seamless flow from room to room. Pale blues and soothing colors were selected to create a true oasis.

Above: The luminous desert sun shines through arched windows in the sitting room of the La Quinta home.

PAYING HOMAGE

In the formal dining room, we paid homage to the Spanish architecture of the home by incorporating an original, late 18th-century oil painting on the focal wall and paired it with a tiered crystal and bronze chandelier. A gilded table lamp dripping in crystals adorns the credenza. By incorporating antique pieces and original art we added character to the newly built Spanish Colonial structure.

ENCHANTING AND UNEXPECTED

The gentleman's office boasts deep teal walls, creating visual depth and a moodiness that allows the wood and gold accents to pop. The champagne-toned gold-leaf wallpaper on the ceiling adds drama and reflects the light from the chandelier.

"WE TRANSFORMED THE PROPERTY INTO A COMFORTABLE AND CLASSIC ESTATE WITH A DESIGN THAT FEELS AS NATURAL AS THE SETTING."

A STUDY OF OLD AND NEW

A soaking tub and polished marble floors contrast with the antique brass sconces and chandelier in the primary bath. The result is a very special home that honors the architecture, landscape, and most importantly, our clients.

HEDGEROW

PHOTOGRAPHY BY NATHAN SCHRODER

When the owners of this home came to us, they were at a turning point in their lives. Their daughter had just graduated from architecture school and they found themselves empty-nesters. Originally hoping to just update a few rooms in their home, it became clear after meeting with them that a full-fledged renovation was a must. Feeling ready for a change, they agreed to the scope of work and we began our process.

Before we began the remodel, it was important to decipher what was working for the family and what wasn't. We spent a lot of time interpreting the floor plan and creating ease of movement. Designing and finishing to a high standard, we selected honed gray limestone for the first floor and wide-plank reclaimed French oak for the second floor. New rich woven silk wallcoverings were installed in the primary suite and floor-to-ceiling marble in the bathroom transformed the space into a luxurious spa-like retreat. With the removal of a wall separating the dining room and formal living room and the addition of a library that was formerly a mud room, the previously choppy floor plan is now light-filled and purposeful. Other than incorporating a handful of the clients' existing art and antiques, all of the furnishings are new—a welcome change for this family in lifestyle and aesthetics.

The level of finish selections, from the flooring to the cabinetry to the lighting, was truly unique to the owners. The furniture is contemporary yet timeless and steeped in traditional craftsmanship. Much of the lighting throughout the house retains a sculptural quality with Asian influences, while the furniture is quite classic.

The design of the home evolved as our relationship with the clients further developed and we discovered all of the beautiful pieces they had collected from their travels that would take pride of place in their home. Every detail is unique to their personality, and this home has given our clients a fresh perspective on the next chapter of their lives.

ODE TO BEAUTY

The formal sitting room incorporates classically modern schemes inspired by the family's far-flung travels. Intricate details and design elements encompassing shape and color add richness to the space.

PERSPECTIVE

With expansive graciousness and purposeful architectural detailing, the living room flows to the dining room. Steel doors with mirrored pathways open up to the courtyard near the entrance of the home and back terrace off the dining room.

TONAL WARMTH

Lighting with subtle brass accents provides an unexpected element of warmth in the kitchen. The breakfast nook boasts an eight-foot-tall built-in display cabinet complete with steel, glass-paneled doors.

A STUDY IN LAYERS

Adding layers of warmth and personality was achieved through textiles, art, and found objects.

SERENE SANCTUARY

An expansive but judicious use of vein-cut marble is seen throughout the main bath. The polished-nickel freestanding bathtub is the crown jewel overlooking the expansive view beyond.

"A LOT OF TIME WAS SPENT ON INTERPRETING THE SPACE AND CREATING ATMOSPHERE. BEFORE WE BEGAN THE REMODEL, IT WAS IMPORTANT TO DECIPHER WHAT WAS WORKING FOR THE FAMILY AND WHAT WASN'T."

CREATIVE DETAILS

Opposite: Our creativity ran wild in the utility room, where we selected a Spanish coffee-and-black–colored floor tile and paired it with a black honed-soapstone countertop.

Above: The two levels of the home are connected by a custom-designed staircase with a black steel railing that lends a sculptural feel to the second-story landing. Archways were added during the remodel to soften the architecture and add dimension.

COLLECTED

With the owners' preferences leaning toward minimalist design, we selected a grass cloth wall mural to act as the focal point of the entryway. An antique console table found in Bali give it an exotic feel.

COLOR STORY

In the study, a brilliant palette of cognac, caramel, and taupe creates a rich and refined setting.

Opposite: The powder room is defined by minimalist restraint and luxurious textures and materials.

NATURAL SELECTION

Opposite: The owners' collection of statues and large terra-cotta urns on the terrace bring interest to the backyard.

Above: Enjoyed year-round, the outdoor spaces act as another room in the warmer months, and beautiful views across the canyon create a sense of spaciousness.

SNUG HARBOR

PHOTOGRAPHY BY NATHAN SCHRODER

When a Newport Beach couple with three children were in need of a team to renovate their new Cliff Haven residence, they looked no further than us to deliver a fresh take on their Mediterranean-style home. The owners exuded their own sense of personal style and were definitive about their likes and dislikes; we happily worked with them to give them everything they wanted and more. Loving the footprint of the original home, they were looking for added sophistication and clean lines that maximized the square footage.

As with any home renovation with great bones, our responsibility was to respect the architecture and retain the elements that initially drew the couple to it. That meant updating the space without it feeling too modern. We began the project by peeling back the layers and carefully removing elements that didn't make sense then added back pieces that fit the family and their lifestyle.

For this close-knit family, it was paramount to design the spaces with intentionality in mind and to create a home that was dedicated to their daily activities. The large, eclectic farmhouse kitchen and rooms off the kitchen get used daily for living, working, playing, and relaxing.

Upstairs, each of the four bedrooms is completely individual and furnished with a combination of existing and new pieces. Each has its own distinct personality, and a playful atmosphere lingers in the air. A calming scheme was achieved with a serene palette of white, soft blue, and gray in the primary bedroom. Meticulously crafted, custom, slat-wood walls finished in classic white enhance the space and add character. At first glance the walls could be mistaken for a striped wallcovering; however, in this case, as with the entire home, attention to detail attributed to an incredible finished product.

Successfully melding the family's everyday interests with practicality, the home offers a snapshot of who they are. A spirit of harmony exists throughout the home and reflects the confident ease of lives well lived.

ARTFUL INCLUSION

A generously sized live edge table serves as a desk in the study, proving both practical and handsome. A brass and hexagonal-cut alabaster chandelier adds a gallery feel.

SPACE SAVER

Opposite: Glass pendant lights with matching round mirrors above the nightstands add symmetry and play well with the masculine flooring.

Above: A built-in desk and a foosball play area makes the most of every inch in the son's bedroom.

LUXURY DEFINED

The lavishly appointed dressing room is outfitted with every imaginable custom treatment—multiple sources of lighting, mirrored doors, organizational spaces, and a crowning crystal chandelier.

OPEN SPACE

The outdoor fireplace provides a brilliant setting for a visual display of olive
oil jars, statues, and birch wood, making it the focal point of the space.

BALBOA ISLAND

PHOTOGRAPHY BY RYAN GARVIN

Historic Balboa Island, a storied stretch of land in Newport Beach, rich in history as a summer getaway since the early twentieth century, provided the backdrop for our clients' newly built beach house. After we completed their main residence just a few miles away, they came to us to design a beach house where they could relax and unwind in an elegant yet no-frills environment. We immediately knew the home would be designed with all the trappings of a summer house and would reflect the colors of the sea.

Working alongside the builder and architect, every decision was made to take advantage of the picturesque setting. The classic Cape Cod architecture and oceanfront location play off one another in a magical way. The sparkling harbor was a natural muse for our design concept, guiding our every move. The conversation begins on the front patio—a gracious seating area just steps from the sand—where we positioned a firepit, comfortable lounge chairs with brightly colored patterned pillows, and a dining table and chairs. It continues in the interiors, where the fabrics selected really make the house and serve the purpose of durability and beauty. Signature white walls in the kitchen keep it light and bright and help illuminate the space while directing the eye outside. Bright pops of color infuse the home, as the owners love shades of sea glass and turquoise.

The oversized sectional easily takes up the majority of the living room and serves as a comfortable place for the family to gather and make meaningful summer memories. Plantation shutters are used upstairs for privacy and allow natural sunlight to enter. The intrinsic beauty of a seagrass wallcovering with watercolor brushstrokes serves as art in the upstairs den. With clean, contemporary lines, the primary bedroom features uncluttered simplicity, making the space feel well edited and warm.

An overall freshness comes alive throughout this home, where every detail is thoughtfully executed. It truly is a family affair and perfectly reflects the owners' waterside lifestyle.

LIVING ON THE WATER

The views from the main living area have a painterly quality. We fully embraced the Balboa Island lifestyle, and nothing does that better than soft sea glass hues mixed with white and sand.

SEA GLASS HUES

We brought the colors, light, and feeling of the ocean into the interiors. Our clients' love for the ocean and the
casually sophisticated style of California is on full display, beautifully blending the indoors and outdoors.

LIGHT TOUCH

Natural elements and a palette of watery blue hues give the open-concept living room, kitchen, and dining area a diaphanous quality and begs one to linger just a little longer.

"THE WHOLE IDEA WAS TO CREATE A BEACH HOUSE WHERE OUR CLIENTS' FAMILY COULD GATHER, WHERE MEANINGFUL RELATIONSHIPS COULD DEVELOP AND SUMMER MEMORIES WOULD BE MADE."

MODERN COASTAL

In the powder room, watercolor-esque wallcoverings enrobe the space,
while a pale blue onyx stone sink levitates above the light oak flooring.

NAUTICAL INSPIRED

Above: Onyx vanities are carried throughout the home for continuity.

Opposite: A nautical blue and white sailboat wallcovering accents all four walls of the son's bedroom.

EASY AND RESTFUL

Opposite: Not shying away from a maritime-inspired theme in the boys' bedrooms, we even brought it into the bedding with pillows from our own line.

Above: A den separating the boys' bedrooms from the primary suite is an ideal place for the children to practice their instruments or sink into the deep sectional to watch a movie.

BREATH OF FRESH AIR

The all-white palette of the primary bedroom was selected to let the sun, sky, reflections, and varying shades of the ocean shine through into the space.

MADE FOR LIVING

The sitting area in the primary bedroom seamlessly blends with the
entire space and embodies the true spirit of transitional coastal living.

"WE WANTED THE DESIGN TO FEEL TIMELESS, RELAXED, AND SIMPLE, WITH THE SUBDUED COLOR PALETTE AND MATERIAL SELECTIONS."

SPA RETREAT

The primary bath has a spa-like quality boasting an oversized shower and a double vanity with a paneled marble mirror.

NATURAL AND TONAL

The primary bath focuses on creating an intentional space inspired by the soothing elements of the sea.

BAY AVENUE

PHOTOGRAPHY BY NATHAN SCHRODER

This newly constructed bayfront getaway for our clients and their three daughters sits on the farthest point of Balboa Peninsula, where the salty sea air is intoxicating. Everything about this home lures you outside and enfolds you in a kind of ocean-filled heaven.

Having previously worked together on multiple projects—including their primary residence in Los Angeles, several beach houses, and mountain homes in Southern California—a high level of trust had already been established between us. A Cape Cod transitional style informed the maritime blue and white theme, and other soothing colors were selected to echo the sky, sea, and sand. The polished metal accents of the hardware and lighting reference nautical influences and create visual continuity.

The kitchen, dining room, and living room make up one large area on the ground floor. Natural light abounds in the kitchen and bounces off the statutory white porcelain island, complementing the clean-lined millwork and cabinetry finished with custom polished nickel hardware. We knew the clients would be entertaining often in the home, so we selected all performance fabrics for ease and durability. When designing this property, our aim was to bring the outside in for the best of both worlds.

The bunkroom transports you to the cabin of a luxury yacht and speaks to the nautical landscape of the home. With ample room for sleepovers, the bunks were a must for the owners and offer a special place for a good night's rest. The third-floor bonus room features a private rooftop deck and doubles as a bedroom, with a custom pullout sofa bed.

Generously proportioned steel windows and doors take advantage of the natural light and proximity to the water. We didn't want the home to feel over-accessorized or styled, so the ocean remains the focal point. Pared-down layers keep everything very clean and light, allowing attention to the meticulously designed and constructed shell of the home. With an eleven-month timeline from construction to completion, the home is smart and effortlessly chic, made to stand the test of time.

JEWEL BOX

Opposite: A beautiful vignette at the base of the stairs allows the opportunity to display vintage ginger jars and nautical inspired artwork.

Above: The powder room is a jewel box that reflects the owners' love of chinoiserie, crystal, and silver.

"THIS HOME WAS METICULOUSLY CONSTRUCTED AND DESIGNED TO BE TIMELESS AND ENDURING."

HEART OF THE HOME

Not surprisingly, the kitchen is the epicenter of the spacious home. A white porcelain
island and continuous backsplash and countertops complement crisp white cabinetry.

PENCHANT FOR THE SEA

Above: A Lucite and polished silver bar cart sits at the end of the kitchen island for ease of entertaining. The contemporary, clean lines tie in with the transitional design of the beach house and add a touch of glamour.

Opposite: The custom white sectional sits on a plush, hand-knotted rug, taking advantage of the bayfront ocean views. The relaxed and comfortable atmosphere captures the essence of the family that occupies it.

"THE BUNKROOM TRANSPORTS YOU TO THE CABIN OF A SAILBOAT AND SPEAKS TO THE NAUTICAL LANDSCAPE OF THE HOME. WITH AMPLE ROOM FOR SLEEPOVERS THE BUNKS WERE A MUST FOR THE OWNERS AND OFFER A SPECIAL PLACE FOR A GOOD NIGHT'S REST."

UTILITY ROOM

The laundry room continues the maritime theme and boasts a Dutch door and vintage iron porthole. The wavy subway tile backsplash has a natural handmade quality to it.

CLEAN LINES

A Carrara white and black basket-weave mosaic flooring accented by an all-white bathroom keeps the space open and light.

ATTENTION TO DETAIL

White Thassos marble and herringbone Calacatta marble complete the bath

in a guest bedroom. A built-in bench takes advantage of every square inch.

PRIMARY RETREAT

The primary bedroom has unobstructed views of the bay, with a magnificent
fireplace and sitting area for those chilly mornings and evenings.

BLACK AND WHITE

Black iron details accent an otherwise all-white bathroom off the den. Classic basket-weave flooring juxtaposes the modern steel shower doors and iron sconces.

"EVERYTHING ABOUT THIS HOUSE LURES YOU OUTSIDE AND ENFOLDS YOU IN A KIND OF OCEAN–FILLED HEAVEN."

PARTNERSHIPS

Bradburn Home

Castelle Luxury

Eastern Accents

Jaipur Living

Kravet

Leftbank Art

Lexington Home Brands

Mirror Home

Napa Home & Garden

Winfield Thybony Wallcoverings

York Contract/
MDC Interior Solutions

Rolls-Royce

And a special thank-you to Hearst Castle and Rolls-Royce for our amazing brand alignments and design collaborations.

THE HAMPTON DESIGNER SHOWHOUSE
LEXINGTON HOME BRANDS

ACKNOWLEDGMENTS

Thank you to all of those who have supported me and have been part of our journey for more than twenty-five years with Barclay Butera Interiors.

Special heartfelt gratitude to my staff for their unending support, immense talent, and tireless dedication. Thank you for choosing to be a part of this family. I am grateful for your expertise and enthusiasm in bringing our vision to life.

SOURCES

Harbor Island

Builder: Andrew Patterson, Patterson Custom Homes

Architect: Christopher Brandon, Brandon Architects

Finishes: Details a Design Firm

Photographer: Manolo Langis

Marigold

Builder: Scott Nicholson, STN Builders, Inc.

Photographer: Nathan Schroder

Arden Road

Builder: Mur-Sol Builders, Inc.

Architect: Robert Tong

Photographer: Ryan Garvin

One Snowmass

Builder: East West Partners

Architect: 4240 Architecture, Inc.

Photography Courtesy of East West Partners

Promontory

Builder: Germania Construction

Architect: Upwall Design Architects

Photographer: Doug Burke

Park Meadows

Photographer: Kate Osborne

Sage Creek

Architectural Finishes and Specifications: Susan Thiel Design

Photographer: Nathan Schroder

Gleneagles

Photographer: Nathan Schroder

Via Strada

Builder: Sunlite Development Inc.

Architecture: Stracts, Inc.

Photographer: Nathan Schroder

Hedgerow

Builder: Scott Nicholson, STN Builders, Inc.

Photographer: Nathan Schroder

Snug Harbor

Photographer: Nathan Schroder

Balboa Island

Builder: Dennis Vitarelli, Vitarelli Construction, Inc.

Photographer: Ryan Garvin

Bay Avenue

Builder: Mur-Sol Builders, Inc.

Architect: Christopher Brandon, Brandon Architects

Photographer: Nathan Schroder

BARCLAY BUTERA SHOWROOMS

Newport Beach, California

1745 Westcliff Drive

949.650.8570

Park City, Utah

255 Heber Avenue

435.649.5540

Corona del Mar, California

2824 East Coast HWY

949.662.1140

WWW.BARCLAYBUTERA.COM

LEXINGTON HOME BRANDS

SHOP BARCLAY BUTERA

Shop all of Barclay Butera's collections as well as his favorite
curated brands, bestsellers, and new arrivals online at:

WWW.SHOPBARCLAYBUTERA.COM

First Edition
25 24 23 22   3 2 1

Text © 2022 Barclay Butera
Photographs © 2022, as follows:
Front Cover: Kate Osborne
Back Cover: Nathan Schroder
Nathan Schroder: 2, 39–49, 107–123, 125–137, 139–153, 155–175, 177–191, 213–233
Lexington Home Brands: 9, 234, 235, 236, 239
David Potter: 4
Manolo Langis: 6–7, 11–37
Ryan Garvin: 51–67, 69, 193–211, 238
Courtesy of East West Partners: 70–77
Doug Burke: 79–91
Kate Osborne: 93–105
Courtesy of Lexington Home Brands, Bradburn Home, Castelle Luxury, Eastern Accents, Jaipur Living, Kravet Inc., Leftbank Art, Mirror Home, Napa Home & Garden, Rolls-Royce, Winfield Thybony Design, and York Contract/MDC Interior Solutions: 235
Marco Ricca: 236

Published by
Gibbs Smith
P.O. Box 667
Layton, Utah 84041

1.800.835.4993 orders
www.gibbs-smith.com

Text by Hannah Berbos
Designed by Phuong Phan
Printed and bound in China

Gibbs Smith books are printed on either recycled, 100% post-consumer waste, FSC-certified papers or on paper produced from sustainable PEFC-certified forest/controlled wood source. Learn more at www.pefc.org.

Library of Congress Control Number: 2021944684
ISBN 978-1-4236-6025-5